DAVID PASTRNAK

HOCKEY SUPERSTAR

BY RYAN WILLIAMSON

First Edition
First Printing, 2019

Book design by Jake Nordby
Cover design by Jake Nordby
Photographs ©: Fred Kfoury III/Icon Sportswire/AP Images, cover, 1, 16, back cover; Fred Kfoury III/Icon Sportswire, 4, 21; Winslow Townson/AP Images, 7; Eric Canha/Cal Sport Media/AP Images, 8–9; City-Press/Getty Images, 10; Alexander Demianchuk/Reuters/Newscom, 13; Matt Slocum/AP Images, 15; Michael Tureski/Icon Sportswire, 18; Gerry Angus/Icon Sportswire, 22, 30; Chris Brown/Cal Sport Media/Zuma Wire/AP Images, 25; Jeff Roberson/AP Images, 27; Red Line Editorial, 29

Press Box Books, an imprint of Press Room Editions.

Library of Congress Control Number: 2019936732

ISBN
978-1-63494-104-4 (library bound)
978-1-63494-113-6 (paperback)
978-1-63494-122-8 (epub)
978-1-63494-131-0 (hosted ebook)

Distributed by North Star Editions, Inc.
2297 Waters Drive
Mendota Heights, MN 55120
www.northstareditions.com

Printed in the United States of America

About the Author

Ryan Williamson is a sportswriter based in the Minneapolis–Saint Paul area. His articles have appeared in various publications across the United States. He lives with his miniature dachshund, Minny.

TABLE OF CONTENTS

CHAPTER 1

A Record-Breaking Night 5

CHAPTER 2

A Love for the Game 11

CHAPTER 3

Breaking into Boston 17

CHAPTER 4

Leading the Charge 23

Timeline • 28

At-a-Glance • 30

Glossary • 31

To Learn More • 32

Index • 32

88
BAUER
BAUER

1 A RECORD-BREAKING NIGHT

David Pastrnak collected the puck and spun around a Toronto Maple Leafs defender. Then he fired a quick backhanded shot. The goalie attempted a kick save, but the puck flew into the net. The crowd erupted as the Boston Bruins took a 1–0 lead.

Pastrnak and the Bruins were hosting the Leafs in the 2018 National Hockey League (NHL) playoffs. Pastrnak's goal came less than six minutes into the game.

Pastrnak makes a move during a 2018 playoff game against the Toronto Maple Leafs.

The Bruins had roared ahead 5–2 by the middle of the second period. When the Leafs gave up the puck near center ice, Bruins winger Brad Marchand sprinted toward the goalie on a breakaway. He missed the shot, and the puck ended up behind the goal. Pastrnak grabbed the loose puck. Then he skated toward the top of the crease and blasted a shot into the back of the net.

As the third period was winding down, Pastrnak glided toward the top of the crease. His teammate delivered a pass from behind the net.

EXPERIENCED SCORER

David Pastrnak's hat trick in the 2018 playoffs wasn't the first of his career. A month earlier, he collected a hat trick against the Carolina Hurricanes. The Bruins were down 4–1 with just ten minutes left in the game. But then they went on a goal-scoring explosion. Pastrnak notched three goals and his teammates scored two more to give Boston a 6–4 win.

Hats rain down onto the ice after Pastrnak's hat trick against the Maple Leafs.

Pastrnak flipped a backhanded shot over the diving goalie.

The fans threw their hats onto the ice to celebrate Pastrnak's hat trick. Boston cruised to a 7–3 win, and Pastrnak finished the game with six points. It was a sign of great things to come for the young right winger.

HAT TRICK

For his third goal of the night, Pastrnak was skating away from the goal. Even so, he twisted his body around and flipped a backhanded shot into the open net.

Reebok
INTERSPORT
AXA
INTER SPORT
3 STEP IT
Reebok
PÅLPLINTAR
LT
96
Reebok

2 A LOVE FOR THE GAME

David Pastrnak was born in the Czech Republic on May 25, 1996. His father, Milan, was a hockey player in Europe. Milan helped David develop a passion for the sport. However, Milan died from cancer when David was a teenager. That loss left David wanting to be a great player to honor his father. He remembered his father's advice to work hard and practice a lot.

David played youth hockey in his home country. But in 2012, he moved to

A 17-year-old David Pastrnak takes part in a game in Sweden in 2013.

Sweden to play in a pro league. He knew that several NHL players from Europe had played in Sweden to develop their skills.

David faced a few challenges at first. He had to get used to a higher level of hockey in Sweden. He also had to learn to speak English and Swedish so he could talk to his teammates. But David quickly settled in, and he thrived on the ice.

David also played for the Czech Republic's Under-18 and Under-20 teams. NHL scouts took notice of his skills, especially his quick shot and speed. However, some scouts worried that David wasn't aggressive enough. They didn't think he could go up against bigger and stronger players in the NHL.

The Boston Bruins believed in him. They selected Pastrnak in the first round of the

David (left) celebrates with his Czech teammates during the 2013 World Junior Championship.

2014 NHL Entry Draft. He was only 18 years old at the time. Many hockey experts thought Pastrnak might stay in Sweden for a while.

MEETING HIS IDOL

David Pastrnak was a long way from home in Boston. But he was excited to have David Krejci on his team. Krejci was also from the Czech Republic. In fact, before the 2014 draft, Pastrnak said Krejci was his favorite NHL player. He said he tried to play like Krejci when he was growing up. The two became friends after Pastrnak joined the Bruins.

That would give him time to build up more strength. But the Bruins brought him in for their summer development camp. He impressed the coaches with his quick feet, fast shot, and playmaking ability. The coaches played Pastrnak at center instead of his normal wing spot. They wanted him to improve as a defensive player.

During the camp, Pastrnak was very energetic. And he was always smiling on the ice. These were qualities that the Bruins wanted in their players.

The team decided to bring Pastrnak on right away. He went to training camp with the

Pastrnak flashes a big smile after being drafted by the Boston Bruins in 2014.

Bruins that fall. Even though Pastrnak was only 18 years old, he was playing for a spot on an NHL roster.

88
BRUINS
BOSTON
CCM
MX3

3 BREAKING INTO BOSTON

David Pastrnak didn't make the Bruins' roster at the beginning of the 2014–15 season. So, he started the season with Boston's minor league team. He wasn't there for long, though. In just 17 games with the Providence Bruins, Pastrnak racked up five goals and 13 assists. The Bruins decided he was ready.

Pastrnak made his NHL debut on November 24, 2014. He had only eight minutes of ice time that night. But coach Claude Julien saw something in him.

Pastrnak competes in the first NHL game of his career.

BAUER
BAUER

Julien put Pastrnak on a line with some of Boston's top players.

Pastrnak played with confidence in his first game. He kept getting the puck to the net. And the other Bruins fed off him, playing hard on offense. Boston ended up losing the game 3–2 in overtime. Even so, the coaches said they liked what they saw from the young rookie.

In January 2015, Pastrnak scored his first NHL goal. And he scored his second goal later in the same game. His performance led the Bruins to a 3–1 win over the rival Philadelphia Flyers.

Pastrnak started shooting the puck more in 2016–17. Not surprisingly, he started scoring

Pastrnak blasts a powerful shot to score a game-winning goal against the Detroit Red Wings in 2017.

more goals. He put the puck in the net 34 times that season. That was more than double his total from the previous season. Pastrnak also came up big when it mattered, scoring six game-winning goals.

Thanks in part to Pastrnak's great season, the Bruins reached the playoffs in 2017. In the first round, Boston faced the Ottawa Senators. Pastrnak had an assist in Game 1, helping the Bruins to a 3–1 win. In Game 3, Pastrnak scored his first playoff goal. It came on the power play, with Boston trailing 3–2 in the second period. Pastrnak ripped a one-timer that blew past the goalie's stick side.

BECOMING PASTA

Many Boston fans know Pastrnak as "Pasta." Pastrnak's father had the nickname when he played hockey, and David took it when he began playing. Some Bruins fans buy shirts that say Pasta on them. In 2019, Pastrnak even had a pasta emoji printed on one of his sticks.

Pastrnak attempts to skate past an opponent during a 2017 playoff game against the Senators.

Unfortunately for Bruins fans, Boston lost the game in overtime. To make matters worse, the Senators eliminated the Bruins in Game 6.

It was a disappointing end to the season. But things were looking up for Pastrnak. In September 2017, Boston offered him a six-year, $40 million contract. That meant Pastrnak would be in a Bruins jersey for years to come.

38
BAUER
BOSTON
38
Bauer
Bauer

4 LEADING THE CHARGE

David Pastrnak continued to improve in the 2017–18 season. He quickly became Boston's go-to player. His Bruins teammates did everything they could to get him open so he could shoot the puck. That strategy paid off. Pastrnak led the team with 35 goals in the regular season.

Pastrnak's success continued into the playoffs. In Game 2 of the first round, he scored six points against the Toronto Maple Leafs. That strong performance helped the Bruins to a series win.

Pastrnak skates with the puck during a 2018 playoff game against the Maple Leafs.

However, the Bruins' success was short lived. Boston lost in the second round to the Tampa Bay Lightning.

In the 2018–19 season, Pastrnak picked up right where he left off. During his first 39 games, he scored 23 goals. That was the second-most of any player in the NHL.

Boston dealt with several injuries during the 2018–19 season. That meant Pastrnak had to step up. And he didn't disappoint. In March 2019, Pastrnak recorded five points in one game against the New York Rangers. During that game, he scored his 16th power-play goal of the season. No Bruins player had scored that many in nearly 20 years.

Expectations were high as the Bruins entered the playoffs. For the second year in a row, Boston faced the Maple Leafs in the first

Pastrnak looks for a scoring opportunity during the 2019 All-Star Game.

round. Pastrnak scored two goals in the series and helped send the Leafs packing.

Next up, the Bruins took on the Columbus Blue Jackets. In Game 5, the score was tied 3–3 with time running out in the third period. That's when Pastrnak ripped a one-timer into the back of the net. Boston went on to win the series in six games.

In the conference final, the Bruins faced the Carolina Hurricanes. Pastrnak notched a goal and two assists in Game 4, helping Boston complete a four-game sweep. For the first time in his career, Pastrnak would be playing for the Stanley Cup.

In the Final, the Bruins squared off against the St. Louis Blues. Boston played tough, and Pastrnak scored two goals in the series. But it wasn't enough. The Blues won the hard-fought series in seven games.

PLAYING FOR HIS HOMELAND

Pastrnak left the Czech Republic at a young age. However, he still represents his home country on the ice. He first played for the Czech national team in 2011, when he suited up for the Under-16 team. He went on to play for the Under-17 team, Under-18 team, Under-20 team, and senior men's national team. In 2014, Pastrnak earned a silver medal at the Under-18 World Championship.

Pastrnak scores a goal against the St. Louis Blues during the 2019 Stanley Cup Final.

Despite the loss, Bruins fans looked forward to watching Pastrnak play for years to come. The Czech star appeared to have many good seasons ahead of him. Fans hoped he could help bring the Stanley Cup back to Boston.

TIMELINE

1. **Havirov, Czech Republic (May 25, 1996)**
   David Pastrnak is born.

2. **Sodertalje, Sweden (2012)**
   David moves to Sweden and begins playing for Sodertalje SK.

3. **Lappeenranta, Finland (April 2014)**
   David stars for the Czech Republic at the Under-18 World Championship.

4. **Philadelphia, Pennsylvania (June 27, 2014)**
   The Boston Bruins take Pastrnak with the 25th pick in the NHL Entry Draft.

5. **Providence, Rhode Island (October 2014)**
   Pastrnak spends the first several games of the season playing for the minor-league Providence Bruins.

6. **Boston, Massachusetts (November 24, 2014)**
   Pastrnak makes his NHL debut. The Bruins lose 3–2 to the Pittsburgh Penguins in overtime.

7. **San Jose, California (January 26, 2019)**
   Pastrnak plays in his first NHL All-Star Game.

8. **St. Louis, Missouri (June 9, 2019)**
   Pastrnak scores a goal in Game 6 of the Stanley Cup Final, helping Boston to a 5–1 victory over the St. Louis Blues. Three days later, the Bruins fall to the Blues in Game 7.

MAP

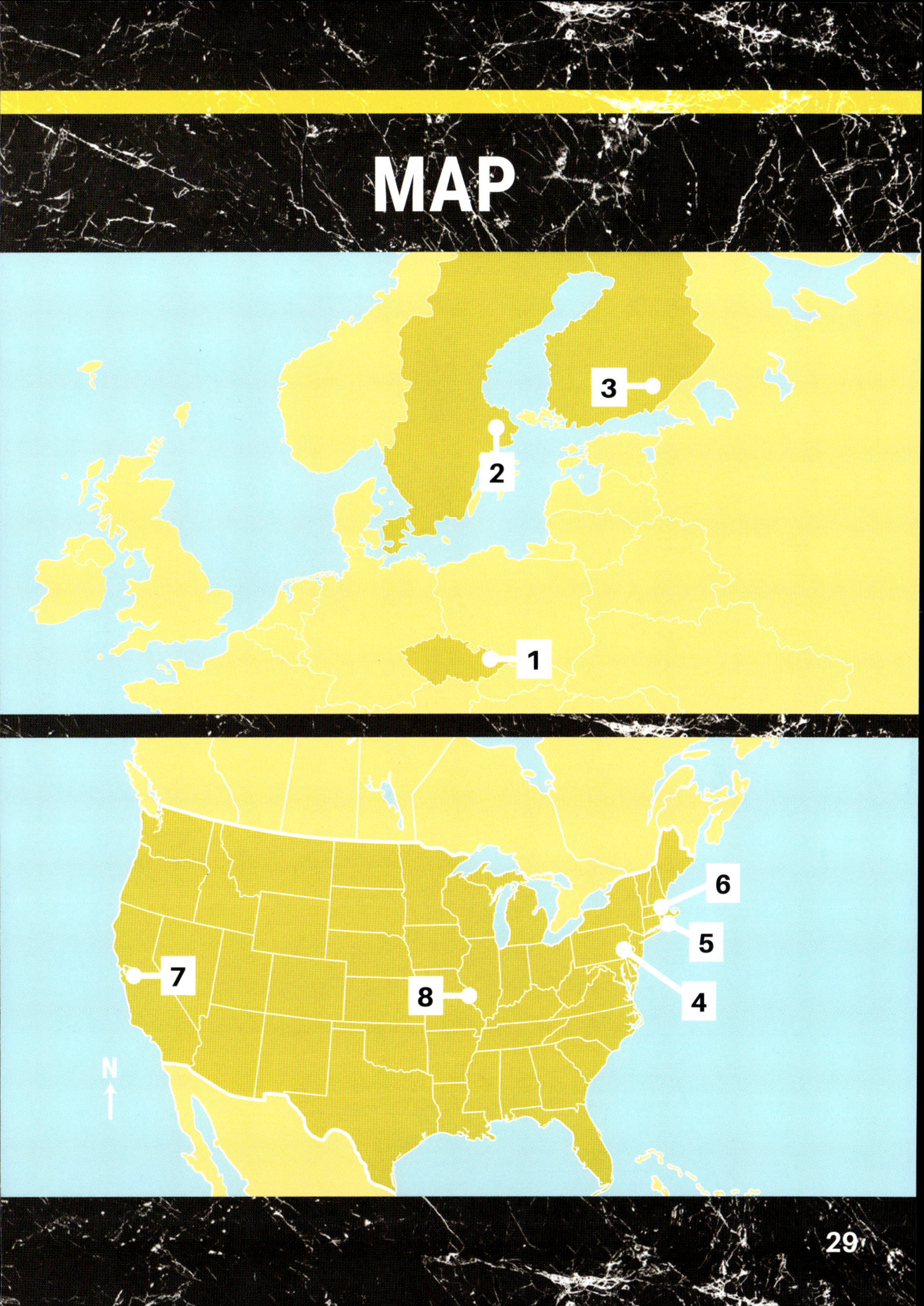

AT-A-GLANCE

Birth date: May 25, 1996

Birthplace: Havirov, Czech Republic

Position: Right wing

Shoots: Right

Size: 6 feet 0 inches, 194 pounds

NHL team: Boston Bruins (2014-)

Previous teams: Sodertalje SK (2012-14), Providence Bruins (2014-15)

Major awards: NHL All-Star (2019)

Accurate through the 2018-19 season.

GLOSSARY

assist
A pass that results in a goal.

backhanded
Using the outside of the stick blade.

crease
The area directly in front of the goalie, painted in blue.

debut
First appearance.

hat trick
A game in which a player scores three or more goals.

point
A statistic that a player earns by scoring a goal or having an assist.

power play
When one team has more players on the ice because of a penalty by the other team.

rival
An opposing player or team that brings out the greatest emotion from fans and players.

roster
An official list of all the players on a team.

scout
A person who looks for talented young players.

TO LEARN MORE

Books

Peters, Chris. *Hockey Season Ticket: The Ultimate Fan Guide*. Mendota Heights, MN: Press Box Books, 2019.

Peters, Chris. *Hockey's New Wave: The Young Superstars Taking Over the Game*. Mendota Heights, MN: Press Box Books, 2019.

Zweig, Eric. *Boston Bruins*. New York: Crabtree Publishing Company, 2018.

Websites

Boston Bruins Official Site
https://www.nhl.com/bruins

Czech Ice Hockey Official Site
http://www.czehockey.cz

David Pastrnak Career Stats
https://www.hockey-reference.com/players/p/pastrda01.html

INDEX

Carolina Hurricanes, 6, 26
Columbus Blue Jackets, 25
Czech Republic, 11–12, 14, 26

Julien, Claude, 17, 19

Krejci, David, 14

New York Rangers, 24
NHL Entry Draft, 13

Ottawa Senators, 20–21

Pastrnak, Milan, 11
Philadelphia Flyers, 19
Providence Bruins, 17

St. Louis Blues, 26
Sweden, 12–13

Tampa Bay Lightning, 24
Toronto Maple Leafs, 5–6, 23–25